THE HISTORY OF EXPLORATION

NORTH AMERICA

New
Forest
Press

Publisher: Tim Cook
Editor: Guy Croton
Designer: Carol Davis
Production Controller: Ed Green
Production Manager: Suzy Kelly

ISBN: 978-1-84898-301-4
Library of Congress Control Number: 2010925461
Tracking number: nfp0003

U.S. publication © 2010 New Forest Press
Published in arrangement with Black Rabbit Books

PO Box 784, Mankato, MN 56002
www.newforestpress.com

Printed in the USA
9 8 7 6 5 4 3 2 1

CONTENTS

EXPLORATION OF NORTH AMERICA — 4–5

THE UNKNOWN LAND — 6–7

THE "INDIAN" NATIONS — 8–9

EVERYDAY LIFE — 10–11

THE COMING OF THE NORSEMEN — 12–13

COLUMBUS — 14–15

COLUMBUS PAVES THE WAY — 16–17

THE TUDOR VENTURERS — 18–19

SPAIN IN NORTH AMERICA: LA FLORIDA — 20–21

THE GOLDEN PROMISE — 22–23

THE FRENCH IN CANADA — 24–25

THE ENGLISH COLONIES — 26–27

EXPLORATION & ENTERPRISE: HENRY HUDSON — 28–29

DANIEL BOONE & THE WILDERNESS ROAD — 30–31

THE SEARCH FOR THE NORTHWEST PASSAGE — 32–33

LEWIS & CLARK: ACROSS THE CONTINENT — 34–35

WESTWARD MOVEMENT — 36–37

THE TRAIL WEST — 38–39

NORTH AMERICA TODAY — 40–41

DID YOU KNOW? — 42–43

GLOSSARY — 44–45

FURTHER READING & WEBSITES — 46

INDEX — 47

ACKNOWLEDGMENTS — 48

Greenland

Atlantic
Ocean

N

SOUTH
AMERICA

1	Bjarni Herjolfsson	11	Álvar Núñez Cabeza de Vaca
2	Leif Eriksson	12	Martin Frobisher
3	Christopher Columbus (1st)	13	Henry Hudson
4	Amerigo Vespucci	14	René Robert Cavelier de la Salle
5	John Cabot	15	Daniel Boone's major travels
6	Juan Ponce de Léon	16	Alexander Mackenzie
7	Giovanni da Verrazano	17	Lewis & Clark
8	Jacques Cartier	18	John Charles Frémont
9	Hernando de Soto	19	Sir John Franklin
10	Francisco Vásquez de Coronado	20	Roald Amundsen

EXPLORATION OF NORTH AMERICA

THE UNKNOWN LAND

When, in 1498, Christopher Columbus finally set foot on the South American mainland, he realized at last that he had found "a very great continent, until today unknown." On his three previous voyages, he had explored the islands and coastline, and it had been his unshakable belief that he had reached the fabled shores of India. However, to its first European explorers, North America was a big disappointment. It was the wrong place at the wrong time; too big, too empty, and too much in the way of their real objective. It was discovered accidentally, and when discovered, it was not wanted. But the lure was strong—knowledge, adventure, wealth, and glory. Many came. Some searched for gold and, finding none, moved on. Some found death and never-ending fame. The French arrived and built a trading empire on fur and friendship. The English landed looking for new lands to colonize, and stayed to make it so. Those who saw that the New World was not just the route to wealth, but the source of it, settled there, bore its many hardships—and created strong new nations. By the beginning of the 1700s, North America's true riches had been discovered: fish and fur; timber and tobacco; waterways and good, rich land. And later, too, there would be gold . . .

THE NEW WORLD

Amerigo Vespucci (1454–1512) was an Italian merchant, navigator, and self-publicist. He said he had made four voyages to the lands in the West. After the first, in 1497, Vespucci claimed to have sighted a huge new continent (South America). After further voyages with Spanish expeditions in 1501 to 1502, he wrote a famous letter calling his earlier discovery *Mundus Novus*, the "New World"—the first person to do so.

AMERICA

Idealized native peoples became the inspiration for European writers and artists, appearing in fanciful form in paintings, illustrations, and sculptures. Engravings like this one were entitled, like so many works of art relating to the New World, simply "America."

A LASTING LEGACY

When the new world maps were drawn by the German cartographer Martin Waldseemüller in 1507, he accepted Vespucci's claims and called the new southern continent "America." Soon the name was used throughout Europe for all the newly discovered western lands. Vespucci may not have been the first to reach the mainland of America, but his name alone has assured his place in history.

THE LANDSCAPE OF IMAGINATION

Like its people, the landscape of North America became a place of fantasy, based on the descriptions of early travelers overawed by its sheer size and the extremes of both its scenery and climate. Early paintings by European artists were often influenced more by their own romantic notions of the New World than by any firsthand experience. To those early artists who *did* travel through the landscape of North America, it was a land of unimaginable beauty. The German-born painter Albert Bierstadt (1830–1902) traveled west with surveying expeditions and painted what he saw. His huge paintings of the Rocky Mountains and the Yosemite Valley are made even more awe-inspiring by the accuracy with which they were observed.

THE NOBLE SAVAGE

From their first contact, the native peoples of the Americas exerted a great fascination over European adventurers and colonists. In person, they were likened to ancient Greeks and admired for the natural simplicity of their lives. The concept of the "noble savage" soon became fashionable throughout Europe. Natives from the Americas were paraded like trophies before their royal patrons by triumphantly returning explorers.

THE "INDIAN" NATIONS

The first people to inhabit the huge lands of North America arrived at the end of the last ice age—around 15,000 years ago. Crossing the narrow land bridge that then joined the northeastern corner of Asia to the westernmost tip of Alaska, they followed game into the untouched lands revealed by the receding ice. Over the centuries, more and more people came. They spread out over the whole of the western hemisphere to the tip of South America. Another group arrived 6,000 years ago and colonized the far north—the Inuit. The immigrants remained in small, separated groups and different ways of life evolved. They became many "nations": some built homes in the northern woods; some founded cities in stone in the desert mountains; some were river-based; while others roamed freely after the buffalo on the great open plains. Customs and cultures grew, based on a close association with the land itself and the creatures that lived on it. By 1491, there were 15,000,000 Native Americans living in what is now the United States and Canada—not very many people for such a huge space. Many welcomed the newcomers, for they had legends of tall, fair-skinned men in flowing clothes, arriving "out of the sea on floating islands covered with tall trees." Myth and reality were about to meet.

WHY INDIANS?

When Christopher Columbus reached the islands of the Caribbean in 1492, he was convinced that he had reached his objective—India. He mistakenly called the lands that he visited the "Indies" and the native peoples "Indians." Five hundred years before, the Vikings encountered natives who loved red so much that they smeared their faces with red ocher from the earth. They called these brown-skinned people the "redmen" or "redskins." Neither name was meant in an insulting way— rather the reverse. The names were widely used in reference to the native peoples of both North and South America, and they became commonly known as American Indians. However, the correct term is Native Americans.

THE ANASAZI

The Anasazi were the prehistoric ancestors of the pueblo Indians of the Southwest. Their civilization lasted from around 200 B.C. to A.D. 1300, during which they built the great cliff dwelling at Mesa Verde. These spears found in Utah date from that period. A very mysterious people, their name in Navajo means "enemy ancestors."

THE FIVE NATIONS

The five Indian nations that formed the Iroquois League were the Mohawk, Seneca, Oneida, Onondaga, and Cayuga peoples of the Northeast. Iroquois legend tells of how the warring nations were brought together by a divine messenger, called the Peacemaker, helped by two tribal leaders, Tsiskonseseh and Aiontwatha. Immortalized in Henry Wadsworth Longfellow's epic poem, Aiontwatha became known as Hiawatha, the Singer of Songs, who calmed the evil Onondaga Chief Atotahoh with a Hymn of Peace. Then Hiawatha combed the snakes from Atotahoh's hair. The Peacemakers turned evil to good by making the strong, but vanquished, Atotahoh a Peace Chief—and the five nations grew strong.

CEREMONY AND RITUAL

The Iroquois sought balance in all things—between people and nature, men and women, good and evil. They used music, dance, songs, and art to create and celebrate this balance. Masks like this one were used in False Face ceremonies to turn away unkind spirits.

JOURNEY FROM THE NORTH

The Indian nations told stories. They built a culture on myth and legend, handed down in painting and crafts, dance and song, and spoken tales of the fireside. They all remembered their northern ancestors, and the history of their beginning became their mythology. The Tewa people of the American Southwest have a song that begins: "Yonder in the North there is singing on the lake. Cloud maidens dance upon the shore. There we take our being . . ." In this contemporary painting, the artist Felipe Davalos celebrates the first migration of the Tewa. As they traveled south, they divided on each side of a great river—the Winter People to the east and the Summer People to the west. Where they joined once again, they built their great pueblo cities.

INDIANS OF THE PLAINS

Life on the plains was a life on the move, following buffalo and the seasons. But there was time for ceremony and clothing for special occasions. Left is a pair of beaded, quilted Sioux moccasins; right, a decorated buckshirt worn by a Blackfoot brave.

EVERYDAY LIFE

Most Europeans found the Native American lifestyle alien, uncomfortable, and sometimes dangerous. Family was considered very important and the women were responsible for the day-to-day running of the family. They maintained the tepee, planted crops, carried out other agricultural work, collected firewood, and made clothing and crafts. Occasionally they would fight. European traders were also surprised when they found themselves doing business with women. Also, the Native American tribes often had very civilized methods of resolving disputes. For example, European governments of the time used punishments to force their subjects to obey, while Native Americans co-operated voluntarily. Individuals were allowed to disagree and go their own way—even if the elders of the tribe recommended war, it was up to each warrior to decide whether to fight or not. There were few punishments—the worst punishment for a Native American was to be banished from their tribe.

EXPOSURE

Life on the Great Plains was particularly hard, as the weather-beaten face of this old Plains Native American woman shows. One result of this was a custom known as "exposure"—sometimes, when the tribe moved on to another camp, they would leave an old person behind to starve. Old people realized that moving on might be the difference between life and death for the rest of the tribe, and often did not want to travel with their families. When the painter George Catlin spoke to one such old man, he was told: "I am a burden to my children and I wish to die."

CHOCTAW ENCAMPMENT

Most Native American tribes were either nomadic or semi-nomadic as in
many parts of North America the weather was too unreliable to rely
on farming. Many tribes spent most of the year living off their
surroundings as hunter-gatherers. In the winter, the Choctaw tribe
of the Southeast prepared the fields and planted crops such as
maize, sunflowers and sweet potatoes. In the summer, they left
to go fishing, and to gather fruits and berries. During this
time they lived in rough, temporary wooden shelters (left).

STORY-TELLING

When the Europeans arrived in
America in 1492, the Native
Americans had no written language.
Much of their leisure-time was spent
listening to stories. This meant the myths
and customs of the tribe were passed
down from one generation to the
next. Sometimes, if a story-teller
was unable to walk, he would be
carried by the young men from
one village to the next, so eager
were the Native Americans to
hear the traditional stories.
In this way, an aged or
disabled person could
play a valuable role.

BEAR HUNT

Native American bows and arrows
were not powerful enough to
bring down a bear, so the hunters
had to kill a bear at very close
range. They went right up to it,
then slipped round under its
paws and stabbed it in the
side. Bear hunting, therefore,
was very dangerous! Before
they attacked, the hunters often
prayed to the beast's spirit, asking
that it give its life to benefit others.

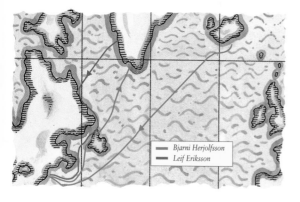

Bjarni Herjolfsson
Leif Eriksson

THE COMING OF THE NORSEMEN

"From the fury of the Northmen, O Lord, deliver us!" For three centuries, the inhabitants of Europe had prayed for protection from the ferocity of marauding Vikings. These tall, fair-skinned warriors would swoop upon their unsuspecting neighbors, carrying off goods, ransom, and slaves. But their greatest need was for land. Leaving their own harsh mountainous homelands, the Northmen roamed the seas in their dragon ships. The Swedes traveled east to Russia, while the Danes and Norwegians sailed west to Great Britain, Ireland, and the islands of the North Atlantic. In A.D. 815, they began a series of migrations, settling first in Iceland where they built successful new colonies, and on to Greenland. But, tough as they were, the settlers found Greenland a difficult place. It was time to set off once again in search of fertile lands. In 1000, Leif Eriksson set out with 35 men to find the lands that Bjarni Herjolfsson had sighted 15 years before. They found Bjarni's land of rocks and ice and named it Helluland (the Land of Rocks). When they stepped on to the barren, rocky shore, Leif said: "Now we have done better than Bjarni . . . we, at least, have set foot on it!" The land they stood on was the coast of Labrador—they had discovered North America.

LEIF ERIKSSON (c. 970–1020)

Erik the Red's son became North America's first recorded explorer. After he and his party made their first landfall, they sailed on south and found a wooded lowland that he named Markland (Wood Land)—now Nova Scotia—and on to a much more fertile coast. They found fish in abundance and berries. Leif named this land Vinland the Good. No one knows exactly where along the coast of North America Vinland lay, but many scholars now believe that it was on the New England coast at Cape Cod.

VINLAND

With Leif Eriksson on his journey of discovery was a German named Tyrker, who had looked after Erik's family when he left Iceland. Wandering off on his own, Tyrker found vines and berries like those he remembered from his childhood in Germany. He told Leif that he had found grapes with which to make wine during the coming winter—thus giving Vinland its name.

ERIK THE RED

In A.D. 982, a Viking chief named Erik the Red was banished from Iceland. He went exploring and found another huge island to the west, whose welcoming fjords and fertile summer valleys inspired him to name it "Greenland," despite the fact that only one-fifth of the land was free of ice.

NORTH AMERICA
-A TIMELINE-

~13,000 B.C.~

First migration of people from Asia across the land bridge into North America

~4000 B.C.~

Inuit colonize far North

~200 B.C.–A.D. 1300~

Anasazi civilization in the Southwest; cliff-dwellings in Mesa Verde

~982–985~

Erik the Red founds the colony in Greenland

~985~

Bjarni Herjolfsson makes the first Viking journey to the North American coast

~1000–1003~

Following Bjarni's route, Leif Eriksson makes landfall on Cape Cod where the Vinland colony is established but fails

AN ACCIDENTAL DISCOVERY

One young settler, Bjarni Herjolfsson, set out with his crew from Iceland to Greenland in A.D. 985. Three days from land, the fair winds died and his ship was carried southward by the current. Drifting into a huge bank of fog, they lost their bearings for many days. When the fog lifted, they lay off the coast of a low, wooded land—not Greenland, which was both mountainous and icy. They sailed north again, passing a rocky island that had a glacier. Bjarni pronounced it "worthless." A four-day gale brought them miraculously to their destination, having visited the coast of North America on the way!

EVIDENCE

A good deal of evidence has been found to prove the presence of the Vikings in North America. Much of it comes from a settlement on the northern tip of Newfoundland, named L'Anse aux Meadows. Its site, on such a storm-lashed coast, suggests that it was a temporary settlement founded by colonists whose ships were swept down the Straits of Belle Isle by the strong Labrador current. Other sites have been found as far north as Ellesmere Island off the Arctic coast of Canada.

13

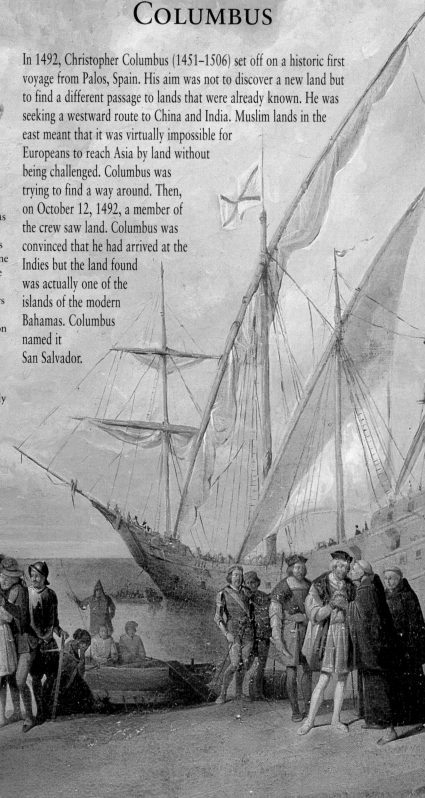

COLUMBUS

EARLY LIFE

Born in the Italian seaport of Genoa, Cristoforo Colombo was the son of a master weaver, but the sea was his passion. He spent nine years learning from the Portuguese, the most accomplished navigators in the world. During those years, his obsession to reach the East was born. At 6 ft. (1.8m) he was tall with red hair, enthusiastic, curious, and impressively single-minded.

In 1492, Christopher Columbus (1451–1506) set off on a historic first voyage from Palos, Spain. His aim was not to discover a new land but to find a different passage to lands that were already known. He was seeking a westward route to China and India. Muslim lands in the east meant that it was virtually impossible for Europeans to reach Asia by land without being challenged. Columbus was trying to find a way around. Then, on October 12, 1492, a member of the crew saw land. Columbus was convinced that he had arrived at the Indies but the land found was actually one of the islands of the modern Bahamas. Columbus named it San Salvador.

EXPERIENCE IN SAILING

After his shipwreck, Columbus stayed on in Portugal and settled in Lisbon. He married, learned to become a mapmaker, and continued his career as a sailor. He visited the west African coast, England, and Ireland. He later claimed that he had sailed to Iceland.

KING JOHN II OF PORTUGAL

It was while he was sailing in the Atlantic Ocean that Columbus deduced that it might be possible to sail westward from Europe to Asia. He first asked King John II of Portugal for help in 1484, but he was refused. The Portuguese were looking for a route to Asia around the African coast.

THE WEALTH OF THE INDIES

Columbus called his plan the "enterprise of the Indies." When medieval Europeans used the word "Indies," they did not mean just India, but also Japan, China, Indonesia, and Southeast Asia. It was believed that these were all very wealthy lands. Using Marco Polo's calculations—the Italian merchant had pioneered a route to the Far East—Columbus figured out that India was around 3,900 mi. (6,200km) west of Europe. In fact, this is about the distance between Europe and the coast of North America.

LA ISABELA

Christopher Columbus had spent seven long years pleading his cause before King Ferdinand and Queen Isabella of Spain. "I plow on," he said bitterly, "no matter how the winds might lash me." He knew that the Spanish rulers were his last hope of realizing his ambition. At last they agreed, thus giving Spain an unexpected advantage in the coming race for power and riches. In honor of his patron, Columbus named his first, short-lived settlement, on the West Indian island of Hispaniola, La Isabela.

THE WORLD AFTER COLUMBUS

Columbus' voyages began a period of European exploration that lasted for 300 years. Long before it was over, geographers claimed that they could now map the whole world. This map, drawn in 1608, incorporates a century of new information about the Americas. It is confidently titled "A new Geographical and Hydrographic Map of All the Known Lands of the Globe."

NEW WORLD PLANTS

Unusual New World fruit and vegetables became much more than curiosities to the first explorers and early settlers. In time, many of the staple plants of the Native Americans—such as maize, potatoes, and tobacco—would be introduced into Europe in the form of both plants and seeds. Others, such as the Cassava root, agave, prickly pear, and pineapple were also introduced with some success. Sweet potatoes were brought back as early as 1493 when Christopher Columbus returned to Spain.

ASTROLABE

An astrolabe is a mechanical working model of the movement of heavenly bodies. By measuring the exact position of the Sun or a bright star, mariners could plot their position at sea. Astrolabes were first used by ancient Greek and Arab navigators. The Portuguese devised an updated version that was widely used by the mariners of Columbus' time.

COLUMBUS PAVES THE WAY

Christopher Columbus did not discover America—that happened 15,000 years before his journey began. He was not the first European to reach the New World—that had happened at least 500 years earlier. Nor, on any of his four voyages, did he ever reach the North American mainland itself—that would happen seven years after his death. What, then, was the significance of the cry of *"Tierra! Tierra!"* (Land! Land!) that rang out from the first of his three small ships in the predawn light of October 12, 1492? By the middle of the 1400s, the idea that Earth was round—and not flat—was generally accepted by scientists and mathematicians. Sailors were more skeptical. But Columbus believed not only that the world was round, but also that he could reach the East by sailing west. He was equally certain that God had "revealed to me that it was feasible to sail . . . to the Indies, and placed in me a burning desire to carry out this plan!" He was right. But how difficult it was. It could only have been accomplished by a man of stubborn self-belief and a navigator of genius. And the consequence of Columbus's mistaken discovery in 1492? It doubled the size of the known world—and changed the course of history.

Columbus landing in South America

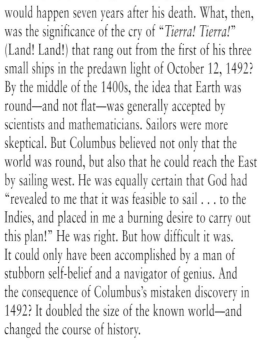

A FAMILY AFFAIR

Several members of the Columbus family took part in the early voyages. His brother, Bartolomé, was in charge of the colony of Isabella during his second voyage. Columbus' eldest son, Diego, served as a page to Prince Juan, heir to the two thrones of Spain. When Columbus died, Diego was named Admiral of the Indies and Governor of Hispaniola.

CARAVELS

The three small ships used by Columbus on his voyage to the New World were caravels, known for being explorers' ships. Designed by Portuguese shipbuilders, the caravel was small, light, fast, and easy to sail. Columbus sailed in three ships: the *Niña* (nickname of the *Santa Clara*), the *Pinta*, and the *Santa Maria*, the largest of the ships. The total crew for all three ships numbered 90 men.

THE TUDOR VENTURERS

SIR FRANCIS DRAKE
(1540–1596)

Much more of an
adventurer than an
explorer, Francis Drake
became one of the most
feared—and successful—
pirates of the 1500s. With
the secret encouragement
of Queen Elizabeth I,
Drake looted the Spanish
treasure ships laden with
gold from the New
World. During several
voyages to the West
Indies in the 1570s,
Drake attacked the
Spaniards on the high
seas and besieged them
in their home ports.

While the Spanish and Portuguese were staking their claims in South America
and likely to control any southern trade routes to the East, other European
monarchs looked north. It was important to both the English and the French
to find what they believed was the key to unimaginable wealth and power—the
shortest trade route to the spicelands of the Orient. King Henry VII of England
decided to do a little exploring of his own, and another Italian was on hand
to help him. John Cabot made two voyages to the New World,
sailing due west from the British Isles. He explored
the coasts of Newfoundland and Nova Scotia,
and touched the North American mainland
before returning home. His claim that he had
reached the "land of the Great Khan" was
mistaken, but his claim to lands in the
name of an English monarch opened the
way for centuries of exploration and
colonization of the eastern coast of
North America—perhaps the most
important discovery of all.

MARTIN FROBISHER (c. 1535–1594)

Frobisher was a contemporary of Drake and one
of the first of the English navigators to make
a true search for the longed-for Northwest
Passage. He made three attempts to reach
Asia by sailing northwest. He failed,
but his voyages greatly extended
geographical knowledge of Greenland
and the northern coast of Canada.
He discovered Frobisher Bay on Baffin
Island. Frobisher was lured away from
the task of further exploration by the
discovery of a golden rock on his first
voyage in 1576. He returned twice more
to fill his ships with the ore—but, alas,
what he had carried back to England
was only fool's gold.

CODFISH AHOY!

"The sea is swarming with fish, which can be taken not only with the net but in baskets let down with a stone . . ." This was how one of the sailors on John Cabot's first voyage described their arrival in the rich fishing grounds off the Canadian coast. Fishing fleets soon followed to create the first major industry in North America. Their logs and records helped mapmakers prepare much more accurate charts for later voyages of discovery.

JOHN CABOT (1450–c. 1500)

Italian by birth and a mapmaker and merchant by trade, Giovanni Caboto brought his young family to Bristol, England in the 1480s, where he became John Cabot, navigator. Inspired by Columbus' voyage in 1492, Cabot set out to search for a northerly route to Asia. He was backed by the English king—who granted Cabot and his sons "full and free authority leave and power . . . to seek out, discover and find whatsoever isles, countries, regions, or provinces of the heathen and infidels . . ." in exchange for one-fifth of all profits. Cabot was financed by the merchants of England's busiest seaport and sailed in the *Matthew* from Bristol in 1497.

NORTH AMERICA -A TIMELINE-

~1451~
Christopher Columbus born in Genoa

~1492~
Columbus' historic voyage across the Atlantic Ocean, landing in the Bahamas, convinced he has reached the Indies

~1497~
John Cabot explores the east coast of Canada

~1501~
Amerigo Vespucci names the western continent Mundus Novus (the New World); his name goes on a map of 1507

~1513~
Juan Ponce de Léon becomes first European to reach North American mainland since the Vikings; discovers La Florida

~1524~
Giovanni da Verrazano explores northeast coast; discovers New York Bay and Narragansett Bay

NEW ALBION

On the orders of his queen, Drake set out in 1577 on his greatest adventure—to sail through the Straits of Magellan and surprise the Spaniards. His task successfully completed, he sailed up the Californian coast as far as Canada, hoping to find a shorter route back to England. Finding none, Drake returned to California for repairs. Laying a somewhat casual claim to the land around the Spanish settlement of San Francisco, he renamed it New Albion. But Drake was no colonist, and "New Albion" lasted hardly longer than his fleeting visit to North America.

NAVIGATIONAL INSTRUMENTS

Tudor explorers were helped on their voyage by several navigational aids such as compasses, solar and lunar dials, and astrolabes. This unusual brass compendium of astronomical instruments was made by Humphrey Cole in 1569.

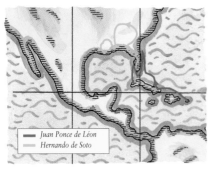

Juan Ponce de Léon
Hernando de Soto

SPAIN IN NORTH AMERICA: LA FLORIDA

The discoveries made by Christopher Columbus gave Spain an important advantage in the exploration of the "Indies"—especially over its old rival, Portugal. By the early 1500s, many more expeditions to exploit the possibilities of the New World were underway. Some were made by people who had sailed with Columbus, such as Juan Ponce de Léon, who colonized and governed Puerto Rico before setting out in 1513 to explore the islands to the north, searching for gold. Instead, he made a momentous discovery and became the first European to stand on the mainland of North America since the Norsemen left 500 years before. But this southern land was very different—lush, green, and tropical. He called it "La Florida." However, in those early days, the main thrust of Spanish exploration was in Central and South America. Inspired by legends of incredible treasure in the lands to the west, the Spanish were spectacularly successful. In a little more than a decade (1521–1533), they had conquered and plundered the great civilizations of Mexico and Peru. Fueled by native legends of El Dorado, the legendary "lost city of gold," their ambitions grew with each successful conquest. It was time to explore La Florida.

HERNANDO DE SOTO

The man who led the Florida expedition was Hernando de Soto (c. 1500–1542), who was one of the richest men in Spain. But he also wanted a seat of power in the New World, and the King of Spain offered him La Florida—to be conquered, held, and governed at his own expense. De Soto accepted, raised an army that was the "youngest, best equipped, and most professional ever to sail from Spain," and landed at Tampa Bay in 1539.

THE SPANISH EMPIRE

By 1600, the Spanish Empire of La Florida was enormous, stretching from the Atlantic Ocean to the Pacific Ocean and from the Gulf of Mexico to Chesapeake Bay. Constantly under attack over the next 200 years, it became part of the United States in 1821.

THE MIGHTY MISSISSIPPI

For three years, De Soto's remarkable army wandered farther into the northern continent than any Europeans had before them, fighting their way through swamps and forests and meeting both welcome and ambush from the native tribes along the way. And always there were tales of the treasures that lay just ahead. At long last, bedraggled and battle-scarred, De Soto and his followers came upon something more important than treasure. On Sunday, May 8, 1541, they stepped out on to the banks of the greatest river that any Spaniard had ever seen. They called it the Rio Grande, but it was already known by its Algonquin name, the Mississippi.

THE NATIVES OF FLORIDA

"The people are thus naked, handsome, brown and well formed in body . . ." John White was one of the first artists to record the New World in the 1500s. He traveled widely and was interested in everything— the plants, animals, and landscape, as well as the life and customs of the native peoples. His drawings provided an accurate study of the people the first visitors met when they landed in the New World.

THE FOUNTAIN OF YOUTH

Like so many of his intrepid countrymen, Juan Ponce de Léon (1460–1521) set out on his voyage northward dreaming of wealth and glory. The Spanish had many legends, but there was one which took his fancy—that somewhere to the north was a magical spring whose pure waters would ensure eternal youth. He may well have found sparkling waters of healthy mineral springs, but what is certain is that he found the land of "Florida"—part of what is now the United States of America.

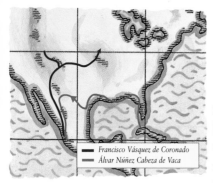

Francisco Vásquez de Coronado
Álvar Núñez Cabeza de Vaca

THE GOLDEN PROMISE

Someone who listened with interest to the tales of golden treasure to be found beyond the mountains of Mexico was Francisco Vásquez de Coronado (c. 1510–1554). Sent by the Viceroy of Mexico, he set out in 1540 to push northward in search of the fabled "seven cities of Cíbola"—a legend of riches that all Spain knew, now given new life by the successful plundering of Mexico and Peru. There must be cities of equal wonder in the unknown lands to the north, and he would find them! For two years, his party was driven onward, through the white heat of the southern desert and up into the Great Plains of present-day Oklahoma and Kansas, but their search was in vain. However, they did find things that no European had ever seen: great open lands of tall grass, large herds of buffalo, and the mysterious pueblo cities of the Zuni. They even stumbled upon a still greater wonder—the Grand Canyon. But they found no gold. Coronado saw his expedition as a failure, later saying, "It was God's pleasure that these discoveries should remain for other peoples." His words might stand as an epitaph for the whole of the Spanish adventure in North America.

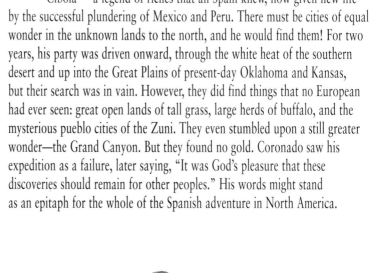

STRANDED

Álvar Núñez Cabeza de Vaca (c. 1490–1560) was a member of an ill-fated expedition to explore the coast of Florida. Shipwrecked in 1528 on the Texas coast, de Vaca and three companions were enslaved by the local tribes for the next five years before escaping. Then they began to walk. They walked across the Mexican Peninsula, reaching the Gulf of California in 1536. They became, by accident, the first Europeans to cross the North American continent from the Atlantic to the Pacific.

CORONADO'S MARCH

Coronado's party was impressive. Joining him on the arduous journey from Mexico were 336 Spaniards and 1,000 native bearers, guides, and interpreters.

CORONADO'S LEGACY

When the first settlers made their way to Texas and New Mexico in the early 1800s, they were astonished to find huge herds of small, tough horses roaming wild on the plains. These were the "mustangs," descendants of the 1,500 Spanish horses that carried Coronado and his party on their journey through the Southwest. Coronado's horses were of Arab blood—strong and intelligent. By training mustangs, the Indian braves became the heirs to the great Spanish tradition of horsemanship—and formidable warriors.

NORTH AMERICA -A TIMELINE-

~1535~
Jacques Cartier discovers the Saint Lawrence River and establishes Montreal for France

~1539–1542~
Hernando de Soto explores the Southeast; discovers the Mississippi in 1541, and dies there in 1542

~1540~
Coronado discovers the Grand Canyon

~1576~
Martin Frobisher searches for the Northwest Passage and discovers Frobisher Bay on Baffin Island

Francis Drake claims Spanish settlement at San Francisco as "New Albion"

~1586–1587~
First English colonies on Roanoke Island in Virginia; none survive

Virginia Dare born 1587

THE GRAND CANYON

Coronado's native guides shared their legends of great cities, huge grasslands, and natural wonders, but the Spaniards only valued gold. Their searches took them through uncharted areas of the Southwest—all claimed for the King of Spain. It was a landscape of stark and unimaginable beauty. At its heart lay the Grand Canyon, created over millions of years by the winding Colorado River cutting its way through the soft, multicolored rocks. It is now 277 mi. (446km) long and almost 1 mi. (1.5km) deep. Even the treasure-seeking Spaniards must have gasped in awe at such a sight.

THE FRENCH IN CANADA

The French, like the English, wanted to find a shorter northern route to the riches of the East. In 1535, the French explorer Jacques Cartier (1491–1557) ventured farther north. Beyond Newfoundland, he came upon an undiscovered waterway. It was a huge river, later called the Saint Lawrence. In small boats, Cartier and his men sailed more than 1,000 mi. (1,600km) deep into the heart of the continent. From a vantage point high above the river rapids, Cartier looked out over a huge land of dense forests and broad inland seas. He named the spot Mount Royal (later Montreal). Cartier's four expeditions allowed France to claim large areas of land, which became known as New France—the heart of the French presence in North America. Cartier, like so many others, was looking for a way *around* the new continent and not at the possibilities to be found within it. But those who followed began to see that true wealth lay in the natural resources of the New World. They created a great trading empire based not on plunder, but on trade alliance with the Native Americans, who dealt in another precious commodity—fur.

GIOVANNI DA VERRAZANO
(C. 1485–1528)

Eleven years before Cartier's expedition, the Italian Giovanni da Verrazano sailed to the New World on behalf of the French king, Francis I. He explored the eastern coast of the new continent, trying to find a passage leading westward. He explored New York Bay and Narragansett Bay—and traveled as far south as Carolina—but the long coastline remained unbroken.

DOWN THE MISSISSIPPI

The motivation for the early exploration of the Mississippi River was mainly for personal gain. But there were others with a wider vision. Réne-Robert Cavelier de la Salle (1643–1687) was obsessed with the idea of creating a chain of linked trading posts along the banks of the Mississippi. He traveled its full length from Quebec to the Gulf of Mexico and back again. In 1682, he claimed the whole of the Mississippi Valley for France, naming it for Louis, his king. The great Louisiana territory was born.

THE INLAND SEAS

In 1608, Samuel de Champlain (c. 1567–1635) founded the first permanent colony in New France at Quebec as a trading outpost. Champlain learned from Native American guides of several large bodies of water that lay to the south and west. He first saw the 120-mi. (200-km) long Lake Champlain in 1609. Following the Saint Lawrence west in 1615, Champlain entered the system of huge lakes now known as the Great Lakes. Later, French explorers threaded their way deep into the Canadian wilderness by following the intricate, interlocking system of waterways, along which trade would flow for centuries to come.

THE ENGLISH COLONIES

THE PEACEABLE KINGDOM

Painted by the Quaker artist Edward Hicks, *The Peaceable Kingdom* reflects his view of the early colonies. The English had a difficult time "taking root" in the New World, but the virtues of fortitude, good sense, honesty, and religious belief helped them succeed. These qualities, along with their language and culture, were the priceless legacy of those first English settlers.

It was some time after Cabot's voyage of discovery for Henry VII that the English began to show serious interest in the New World. Sir Walter Raleigh, flamboyant favorite of Queen Elizabeth I, sponsored three attempts to establish a permanent English settlement. The first two attempts to Roanoke Island in Virginia were unsuccessful, as the colonists found poor land and seas too shallow for good fishing. In 1587, a third expedition sailed for Chesapeake Bay farther north, led by the artist John White and his family. The ship's captain refused to sail north and once again put the 117 colonists down at the ill-fated Roanoke site. Twenty-seven days later, John White's daughter Eleanor gave birth to the first English child born in America—named Virginia Dare. White went back to England for supplies, but when he returned, the colony had vanished. White and his men found the word "CROATOAN" carved on a tree—it was the name of a friendly Native American tribe. No trace of the Lost Colony was ever found, and Roanoke was abandoned. In 1607, English colonists reached Chesapeake Bay at last and established, in this more temperate land, the first permanent English colony at Jamestown, named in honor of the new king.

THE TOBACCO ECONOMY

The Virginia colony had among its members people with the skills to create a new community. In John Smith (1580–1631), they found a leader with common sense. He insisted that everyone worked and established a "tobacco economy," with a tithe of each crop used to support projects for the entire community. It was the first local tax levied in the colonies and helped Jamestown to be self-sufficient.

PLIMOTH PLANTATION

The first English colony in what became New England—the heart of English North America—was founded when pilgrims accidentally landed on a low wooded spit of land just as winter was drawing in. What they had found was a good land, just as Leif Eriksson had found it 600 years before—and having nowhere else to go, they stayed, survived, and prospered.

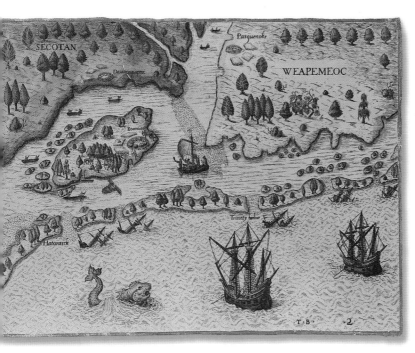

VIRGINIA

This map, or "platt," of the "South Part of Virginia" was painted on vellum by Nicholas Comberford in 1657. It shows in some detail the area of the coast surrounding Roanoke Island—the site of the first English colony in North America—as well as Albemarle Sound, Pimlico Sound, and the long, thin islands of Cape Hatteras. In 1673, Charles II made this area a part of the new colony of Carolina. It is now part of the distinctive coastline of North Carolina.

ARTIST OF THE NEW WORLD

The English artist John White was a member of the first of Raleigh's expeditions to Virginia. He was an enthusiastic colonist and was expected to use his skills to attract other settlers to the new colony. His numerous drawings and delicate watercolor paintings are naturalistic and well observed. White chose to concentrate on the more domestic aspects of Native American life and customs, as in this depiction of the Village of Secoton (left), painted in 1587, with its well-ordered fields and neat huts. The inhabitants danced in a formal ceremony around posts "carved on the topps lyke mens faces."

THE *MAYFLOWER* PILGRIMS

The *Mayflower* sailed from Plymouth, England on August 15, 1620. After its companion ship *Speedwell* began to leak, the *Mayflower* continued on alone across the Atlantic Ocean. It carried 102 passengers, many of these religious reformers. They were heading toward Chesapeake Bay and the colony at Jamestown but made landfall instead at Provincetown on Cape Cod on November 21, 1620. Exploring the coast, they chose a site for a new colony, which they called Plimoth.

EXPLORATION & ENTERPRISE: HENRY HUDSON

THE HUDSON'S BAY COMPANY

Henry Hudson (c. 1550–1611) gave his name to the most influential trading company of all—the Hudson's Bay Company. With this seal from a charter granted by King Charles II of England in 1670, the company was given sole rights of trade and commerce over the whole of the basin of Hudson Bay.

The "Company of Adventurers" embarked upon an enterprise of unparalleled vision and, in the process, created a nation. For the next 200 years the Hudson's Bay Company governed Canada.

By the beginning of the 1600s, the exploration of North America had become an increasingly commercial affair. In place of the haphazard adventures undertaken by mercenary dreamers backed by rulers looking to enhance their power came well-planned expeditions financed by groups of speculators and serious trading companies. What had been a chaotic every-man-for-himself scramble for personal gain and glory became a business opportunity. Yet the one thing that *all* the new backers wanted to find was the Northwest Passage. Between 1607 and 1611, the explorer and sea captain Henry Hudson made four voyages to North America, which took him to within 690 mi. (1,100km) of the North Pole—farther north than any other European had ventured. His attempts to find a navigable westward passage failed, but he discovered the true reason why the route to the East might never be found—ice! Hudson's journeys were of crucial importance for the future of the two countries—the Netherlands and England. Hudson was hired by trading companies in both countries: his discovery of the Hudson River gave the Dutch their first real foothold in North America; his final voyage enabled England to claim both the Hudson Strait and the huge inland sea known as Hudson Bay.

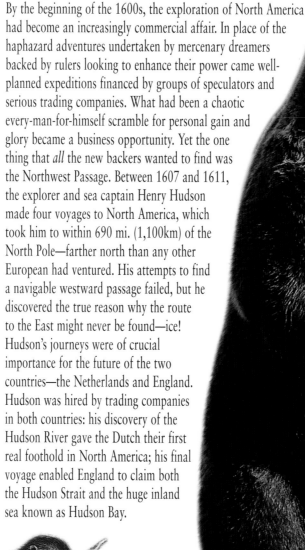

LANDFALL!

Henry Hudson undertook his third voyage for the Dutch East India Company and landed at the mouth of the Hudson River in 1609. Disappointed by his failure to find a northern route that would link them with their interests in the East, the Dutch abandoned further exploration. They did, however, claim the land that he explored on his journey southward along the Atlantic coast—including the Hudson River Valley and the site of what would become New Amsterdam (later New York).

FAMILIAR AND EXOTIC ANIMALS

Many of the animals that European explorers found in the North American woodlands would have been familiar—wolves, grizzly bears (left), foxes, as well as the beavers (far left), which were so greatly prized for their luxuriant fur.

TRADING POSTS

Built on trade alliances with Indian fur trappers, the Hudson's Bay Company built a network of trading posts known as Houses, or Forts. The terms of trade were set in brass tokens linked to the value of a beaver skin. In some areas, goods could be paid for with the Company's own pound notes!

ALEXANDER MACKENZIE (1764–1820)

The huge area of western Canada was opened to traders and settlers as a result of expeditions made by the Scottish explorer Alexander Mackenzie. Beginning at Lake Athabasca in the center of the Canadian wilderness, Mackenzie traveled by water to Great Slave Lake and out on to the broad river that bears his name. Convinced that the westward-flowing river would carry him to the Pacific Ocean, Mackenzie was dismayed when it began to curve northward. He called it the "River of Disappointment." Nevertheless, he traveled the whole of its length, finally sighting the Arctic Ocean in 1789, having traveled 1,054 mi. (1,700km). Mackenzie eventually crossed the continent from east to west in 1793.

DANIEL BOONE & THE WILDERNESS ROAD

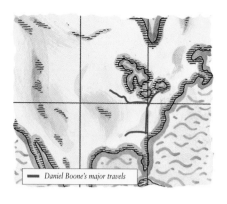

Daniel Boone's major travels

Once the English colonies on the eastern seaboard began to thrive, more and more settlers arrived to make new lives in North America. For more than a century, they poured into the lands governed by the English Crown—lands that lay between the Atlantic Ocean and the great spine of the Appalachian Mountains, running from New England to the Georgia forests. What lay beyond was a matter for speculation: dense, uncharted woodlands, wild beasts, and Native American tribes of uncertain temper? Perhaps even the Pacific Ocean? The pressure for more and more land for settlers was growing, and in spite of English disapproval, people began to think about "going west." It was Daniel Boone (1734–1820) who showed them the way. He was born in Pennsylvania into a family about whom it was said: "They had an itching foot. Something called. Something beyond the mountains always whispered." In 1775, after years of wandering through wilderness that no white man had ever entered, Boone led a party of 30 woodsmen across the mountains. They cleared and connected a complex network of Native American trails and animal pathways to cut the first road leading from the Virginia colonies across the mountains to the Tennessee River Valley and on to Kentucky. Almost 300 mi. (500km) long, it became known as the Wilderness Road. It was the gateway to the west.

AN EARTHLY PARADISE

Once Boone saw the wild wooded hills of Kentucky, he was determined to bring his family there to live in this land he called a "second paradise." By 1800, more than 200,000 pioneers had followed Daniel Boone down the Wilderness Road.

HUNTIN', TRAPPIN', AND WANDERIN'

Daniel Boone spent many years of his life following these three favorite pastimes. To enjoy them, he needed very few things: a good flintlock rifle, a hunting knife, and a strong hunting bag made of macramé and leather in which to carry game. Boone "wandered" a good deal—as far south as Florida and westward into the Missouri Valley. In 1769, Boone and a few hunting companions crossed the Appalachian Mountains at Cumberland Gap (discovered in 1750 by Dr. Thomas Walker) and down into Kentucky. It was a hunting trip that became a two-year exploration of a huge area of the wilderness that lay beyond the mountains—where the Old West began.

THE FRONTIERSMAN

Daniel Boone's son Nathan described his father as being "five feet eight inches high, with broad shoulders and chest . . . (weighing) about one hundred and seventy-five pounds . . . eyes blue and skin fair." Certainly a well-grown and attractive man for his time, but so great was his reputation that he was often described as being huge in stature. In spite of its obvious dangers, his tough frontier life was a healthy one and he lived to the remarkable age of 85. His sharp sense of humor must have helped, too! When the traveling painter Chester Harding came to paint his portrait in the last year of Boone's life, he asked the famous woodsman if he had ever got lost in the forests: "No," answered Boone, "I can't say that I was ever lost, but I was *bewildered* once for three days."

~1600~

Spanish empire of La Florida largest in North America

~1607~

First English colony at Jamestown on Chesapeake Bay; John Smith is leader and the colony survives

~1608–1615~

Samuel de Champlain founds Quebec Colony; discovers Lake Champlain and Great Lakes

French establish fur trading empire in Canada

~1609–1611~

Henry Hudson searches for Northwest Passage; discovers Hudson River, Hudson Strait, and Hudson Bay

~1620~

November 21: Mayflower pilgrims land at Provincetown; they establish Plimoth Plantation

~1670~

Hudson's Bay Company created by Royal Charter

~1679–1682~

De la Salle explores Mississippi valley; claims it for France, and it becomes Louisiana Territory

~1775~

Daniel Boone creates the Wilderness Road

~1776~

Declaration of Independence—13 colonies win their independence from Great Britain

~1793~

Alexander Mackenzie follows the Mackenzie River to the Arctic Ocean

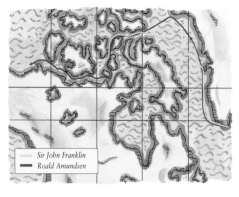

Sir John Franklin
— *Roald Amundsen*

THE SEARCH FOR THE NORTHWEST PASSAGE

The Holy Grail of North American exploration for 500 years, the Northwest Passage defeated generations of geographers, navigators, and "Arctic experts" from all over Northern Europe. But no nation tried so hard and risked so much as the English in their persistent quest. For 300 years after Frobisher's voyages in the 1570s, English mariners continued to push their way north, through the icy seas, and along the inhospitable coast of North America. Continually seeking that perfect route across the top of the world that would give them access to the East, they explored every part of the Canadian Arctic. As the French and English began to explore and colonize the lands that they had claimed, the huge continent became less of a hindrance and more of an opportunity. Interest in finding the Northwest Passage appeared to dwindle—until the early 1800s. The most famous and tragic of these adventures was the third expedition made by Sir John Franklin in 1845. After two successful ventures, he returned to the Arctic, determined to find, at long last, a way through the icebound straits from east to west. In fact, the expedition achieved its objective, but their success remained unknown for a decade. There was no one left alive to tell the tale.

THE REWARD

In 1817, British Parliament offered a reward of £5,000 ($7,000) to the first ship to cross longitude 110° West, north of the polar circle. The challenge was taken up by John Ross the following year, but his two ships were unable to defeat the pack ice. Ross's second-in-command, Edward Parry, made another attempt. This time, as he set off by sea, he sent John Franklin (1786–1847) overland from Hudson Bay to the coast. Parry set out in May 1819, crossed the 110° line and won the reward. Franklin continued on and surveyed the Arctic coast for three full years—a journey of around 5,500 mi. (8,800km). Their discoveries made accurate mapping of the northern coast of Canada possible.

LOST FOREVER!

In 1845, Sir John Franklin set out on his most ambitious voyage. With 129 companions, he sailed in *Erebus* and *Terror* to find the Northwest Passage. Nothing was heard from the expedition, and so, with hope fading for the safe return of her husband, Lady Franklin appealed to the British Admiralty for help. With their backing, and that of the President of the United States, a great search was launched in 1847. It lasted more than ten years and involved 40 ships. Finally, in a cairn of rocks on King William Island, the crew of the *Fox* found Franklin's last message telling of their cruel fate.

THE LAST DAYS

Abandoning the icebound ships, the men had walked for 155 mi. (250km) eastward toward the open sea. *Erebus* and *Terror* were never found. Their last days were commemorated in this painting by W. Thomas Smith, dramatically titled *They Forged the Last Link with their Lives*.

SUCCESS!

The Norwegian explorer Roald Amundsen (1872–1928) spent two years (1903–1905) living among the Inuit of King William Island, making notes and taking measurements. When he was ready, Amundsen and a party of six set out on August 13, 1905 in an old fishing boat, the *Gjoa*. They sailed westward through the straits until they came to open sea. The Northwest Passage had been conquered by boat, but by then, it was almost too late. Within ten years, the Panama Canal was built. It would carry ships loaded with goods and passengers quickly from one great ocean to the other, fanned by tropical breezes rather than icy Arctic winds.

BANNER OF HOPE

Sir John Franklin was fortunate to have a determined and devoted wife who refused to give up the search for him. As well as sending ships to the rescue, Lady Franklin embroidered this flag, carried by the HMS *John Barrow* as it journeyed north. It is a symbol of her unceasing efforts to learn of the fate of the expedition.

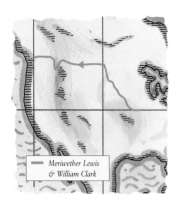

LEWIS AND CLARK: ACROSS THE CONTINENT

Your mission is to explore the Missouri River, and such principal stream of it, as by its course . . . may offer the most direct and practicable water communication across this continent, for the purposes of commerce.
Thomas Jefferson, U.S. President, June 20, 1803

With this formal commission, Thomas Jefferson, third president of the United States, set in motion the first real phase of exploration under the government of the new republic. One year later, the Corps of Discovery set out on its daunting but successful three-year mission—to explore and survey the land west of the Mississippi. The huge Louisiana Territory had changed hands several times, with all the land east of the Mississippi given to the new United States after the War of Independence. By 1801, the remainder had fallen into the hands of Napoleon. Jefferson distrusted the French emperor and concluded what must rank as one of the smartest property deals in history—in 1803, he made the Louisiana Purchase for just $16,000,000, more than doubling the size of the United States. Now the land was his, he wanted an expedition to explore it. He entrusted the task to his young secretary, Captain Meriwether Lewis. With him went Lieutenant William Clark. It was the mission of a lifetime.

NORTH AMERICA -A TIMELINE-

~1803~

Thomas Jefferson concludes the Louisiana Purchase with France

~1804–1806~

Lewis and Clark expedition crosses the continent from Missouri to the Pacific Ocean

~1806~

Zebulon Pike maps territory from Missouri to Colorado

~1819–1822~

Edward Parry and Sir John Franklin explore the Arctic, crossing 110° line and covering 5,500 mi. (8,800km) of coastline

~1842~

John Charles Frémont makes a full survey of region, from the Rocky Mountains to the coast

~1843~

Westward movement begins as settlers set off on the Oregon Trail west

~1845~

After finding route of Northwest Passage, Franklin's expedition is lost; ten-year search organized by Lady Franklin

THE NATURALIST AND THE GEOGRAPHER

Throughout their 7,700-mi. (12,400-km) journey, both expedition leaders took detailed notes of their surroundings. Meriwether Lewis (1774–1809) was the naturalist, noting the richness and diversity of the plant and animal life (right). William Clark (1770–1838) was an excellent draftsman, cartographer, and geographer, who kept detailed notes of all physical features of the journey in his carefully prepared journals.

THE CORPS OF DISCOVERY

Led by army officers Lewis *(left)* and Clark *(right)*, the 45 members of the Corps of Discovery included men with experience in many other trades useful on the long journey ahead. There were carpenters, smiths, hunters, hide curers, and tailors, as well as experts in the universal sign language of the Plains Indians. They left nothing to chance—building camps in which to winter, and designing a special flat-bottomed keelboat, which could be rowed, sailed, or poled.

ACROSS THE ROCKIES

Setting out from the Saint Louis camp in May 1804, the expedition followed the broad Missouri River north into the lands of the Dakotas. There they wintered to harden themselves in preparation for the push across the Rockies, and to forge friendly alliances with Native American tribes. Lewis and Clark knew that their success and safety would depend upon the friendship of Indian braves. And so it proved—again and again "Long Knife" (Lewis) and "Red Hair" (Clark) had reason to be grateful for their help. In the summer of 1805, they carried their boats over the Rocky Mountains and followed the Columbia River to the sea. That November, they reached the Pacific Ocean.

SACAGAWEA

Passing through Native American country, the expedition relied heavily on its French guides and interpreters, George Drouillard and Toussaint Charbonneau. With him came Charbonneau's young Native American wife and her baby son as a sign that this was not a war party. Sacagawea was a Shoshone who had been captured by raiders as a girl. In the summer of 1805, as they moved closer to the Rockies—Shoshone country—the land became more and more familiar to her. The expedition needed to purchase Shoshone horses to take them across the mountains. When at last they met with a party of warriors, Sacagawea recognized her own people. She came forward to interpret before any threat could be made. A tense moment turned into one of joy, their chief was her own elder brother—Sacagawea had come home.

THE PATHFINDER

John Charles Frémont was a captain in the U.S. Army Topographical Engineering Corps who explored and surveyed much of the huge area west of the Rockies. He charted the Oregon Trail—the longest, and toughest, of the great overland routes used by pioneers in the great westward expansion of the United States in the mid-1800s. In 1842, Frémont made the first full survey of the Wind River chain of the Rocky Mountains, making the first ascent of what would later be named Frémont Peak. He later mapped both Nevada and California. His surveys were so important in the mapping of the American West that Frémont became known as the "Pathfinder."

THE VANISHING AMERICANS

"I'm all Injun but my hide," wrote Charles Marion Russell (1864–1926), the American painter who, more than any other, celebrated the Native Americans of the Plains as their way of life changed with the settlement of the West. At the age of 15, the young Russell left his home in Saint Louis to share the lives of cowboys and Native Americans for the next 30 years. His paintings have vitality, accuracy, and an unsentimental sympathy. He worked from an insider's understanding and created a body of work that paid homage to all the people who lived closest to the land. A note on one of Russell's Native American studies read, "This is the only real American. He fought and died for his country—today he has no vote, no country, and is not a citizen, but history will never forget him."

WESTWARD MOVEMENT

KIT CARSON
(1809–1868)

The success of the Lewis and Clark expedition to cross the continent from St. Louis, Missouri, to the Pacific coast had far-reaching consequences. More surveying expeditions were mounted and by 1840 the world began to realize just how vast the new continent was—stretching for more than 2,796 mi. (4,500km) from the Atlantic to the Pacific, and 1,553 mi. (2,500km) from the Great Lakes to the Gulf of Mexico. There was land enough for everyone! Settlers once again set out from the crowded eastern seaboard to take up the challenge of a new life in the West. The Conestoga Wagons began to roll and the pioneers were on the move. Their lives would become the stuff of legend. Their fortitude in the face of enormous hardship and danger became one strong strand in the story of "how the West was won." The "winning" of the West by white settlers—farmers, sheepherders, and cattlemen— meant the division of land, ownership of grazing, and, worst of all, fences. It meant the end of a centuries-old way of life for the Native Americans.

During his travels to the Rockies, Frémont met Kit Carson, who became his official guide for the later expeditions. A great character, Carson was small, tough, and indefatigable. He became a famous Long Hunter, Native American fighter, and explorer of the lesser-known areas of the uncharted West. He fought in the Civil War (1861–1865) in full general's uniform but preferred his comfortable fringed buckskins. It is said that, at the end of his life, Kit ate a prime steak, drank a bowl of coffee, puffed on a final pipe—and died.

THE TRAIL WEST

The great westward movement carried the settlers across the country to California and Oregon—following the Santa Fe and Oregon trails west. They were joined by thousands of new immigrants from northern Europe—Scandinavian, German, Dutch, and Irish settlers joined the great wave of people moving west. In 1870, the population of the territory west of the Mississippi River was 7,000,000; within 20 years, it had risen to more than 17,000,000. Always looking for a better life, these new settlers were constantly ready to move on, to take a chance on the unknown. No longer rooted in the place where they were born, they identified themselves with the entire country—becoming truly "Americans." Oregon was given to the United States by Great Britain in 1846, and the final part of the old Spanish territories won from Mexico in 1848. In 1890, the United States Bureau of Census officially reported that there were "no frontiers left." So America had fulfilled its Manifest Destiny to control the whole of its continental territory from "sea to shining sea." The great age of North American exploration was over.

ZEBULON PIKE
(1779–1813)

Pike mapped the territory from Missouri southwest to the Rockies and gave his name to the highest peak in 1806.

THE CONFLICT BEGINS

During the Expansion Era, eastern Native American tribes were forced to move to lands beyond the Mississippi River. The hunting grounds of the Great Plains became grazing lands for cattle. The Indian nations suffered great hardship and loss as they left their tribal homelands and moved onward toward an uncertain future. While the pioneers were spurred on by the promise of new lands, the Native Americans journeyed because of the loss of theirs. It was a recipe for conflict.

LITTLE WOLF (1820–1904)

A Cheyenne Chief, Little Wolf, became one of the leaders of the Native American resistance to the white settlement of the West. He spent much of his long life at war, escaping death many times.

THE OREGON TRAIL

Urged on by the claims of land promoters to come and settle in the "loveliest country on Earth," thousands of settlers set off from Independence Missouri to travel the 1,860-mi. (3,000-km) Oregon Trail to the Pacific Ocean. Huge trains of wagons with horses, livestock, and families assembled for the journey—most of which would be accomplished on foot by these hardy and determined people. In 1843, the first big migration began when 900 settlers, with all their worldly belongings, left Missouri. Thousands more followed every year. The beauty of the landscape that they traveled through was undeniable. But its grandeur could not mask the danger and hardships, and many people never reached their journey's end.

KANSAS LAND OFFICE

In May 1862, the U.S. Congress passed the Homestead Act. Under the Act, settlers could claim free title to 161 acres (65 hectares) of public land in the western states. In return, they had to stay and cultivate the land for five years. This gave a final boost to the "land rush," as 500,000 families accepted the government's offer before 1900.

HEADING FOR A NEW HOME

The covered wagon—its trademark white canvas cover stretched tightly over wooden hoops—became a powerful symbol of the westward movement. Stoutly built, these wide-bodied vehicles were both transportation and home for many long months. Pioneering families carried all their possessions with them on the journey to Oregon or California. Tight enough to float and tough enough for the harsh terrain, the Conestoga Wagon and its hard-pulling oxen carried many thousands of settlers to a new life in the West.

North America Today

North America has been settled by people from so many parts of the world that there is a huge variety of cultures and religions living on this continent. The people live in a varied range of environments, from frozen areas in the north, such as Greenland and Alaska, to the Mojave desert in California. There are more than 307,000,000 people living in the U.S. today. Every year, one million immigrants from around the world begin new lives in the U.S. However, 12.7 percent of the population live below the poverty line. Canada is the second largest country in the world, in terms of area, but there are only around 33,311,400 people living there today. The "literacy rate" is the number of people aged 15 and over who can read and write. In the whole of North America, the literacy rate is 95.6 percent.

THE INUIT OF NUNAVUT

The Inuit live in a part of the Canadian Northwest Territories called Nunavut, which means "our land" in Inuktitut, the Inuit language. Inuit people live modern lives in many ways, using snowmobiles, telephones, and computers. But some Inuit families, with government help, have chosen to become full-time hunters. They live in camps on the ice. They combine some modern comforts with a more traditional way of life. The Inuit hunt seals, walrus, whales, and wild reindeer for meat and fur. Inuit people do not actually live in igloos—these are only temporary snow shelters built by hunters. "Igloo" means "house" in Inuktitut.

PEOPLE OF QUEBEC CITY

Canada is a country of English- and French-speaking cultures. Quebec City is in the southeast of Canada. Most of Quebec's residents are French-speaking. Vieux Québec ("old Quebec," left) was made a World Heritage site in 1985. It is a maze of streets, ramparts, churches, and old battlefields. It is the oldest city in North America, as well as the only fortified city. Four million tourists visit the city every year so many people are employed in the tourist industry. Quebec City has a population of 638,000 people.

THE CREE OF CANADA AND THE U.S.

The Cree live in Canada—in Manitoba and Saskatchewan. They also live in the U.S.—in Montana and North Dakota. The Cree first lived in forests and wooded swamps, where they hunted, fished, and trapped game. Many still do this today. By 1800, Cree bands (groups) had moved onto the plains to hunt buffalo. Today, the Cree keep the old traditions alive. Cree bands hold "walking out" ceremonies for children to mark the importance of their heritage. The children walk out of ceremonial tepees in their Cree costumes, carrying symbolic tools or goods. There are 200,000 Cree people in all and 100,000 Métis, who have a mix of Cree and French Canadian ancestry.

LIFE IN NEW YORK CITY

New York is the U.S. center for finance, communication, culture, and fashion. Many New Yorkers work in these sectors. People from all over the world have migrated to the U.S., arriving by ship from across the Atlantic. As they sailed into New York Harbor, they passed one of the city's most famous landmarks—the Statue of Liberty (right). New York City has the largest city population in the U.S.—more than eight million people.

GREENLANDERS

Greenland is the world's largest island. Greenlanders are descended from Inuit groups and Scandinavians. Most Greenlanders live in towns along the southwestern edge of the island. The picture *(right)* shows the town of Ilulissat which is on the west coast of Greenland. Ilulissat is Greenland's most popular tourist destination. Although there are roads, most long-distance trips are made by air. There are more than 200 species of fish and other seafood in the island's waters and the fishing industry provides 95 percent of Greenland's income. Greenland's national costume for women is pants worn with high boots—white boots for young girls, red for married women, and blue or yellow for older women.

DID YOU KNOW?

How America got its name?

America was named after the 16th-century navigator and mapmaker Amerigo Vespucci. Of Italian birth, in 1508 he was created Chief Royal Pilot of Spain. All Spanish captains had to provide him with full details each time they undertook a new voyage so that he could constantly amend and update his collection of sea charts. He made several voyages to the New World himself (notably in 1499–1500) and was once credited with discovering America. Although this was not true, he was the first to consider it to be an independent continent and not part of Asia. It was afterward known as "Amerigo's Land" in honor of him.

Why the Atlantic Ocean was called the "Sea of Darkness" by the Arabs?

The Atlantic Ocean was distrusted by mariners for its fearsome winds and sudden storms. It was known to the Arabs as the "Sea of Darkness." The 12th-century Arab geographer Al-Idrissi said of it: "No one knows what is in that sea, because of many obstacles to navigation—profound darkness, frequent storms, unimaginable monsters . . . and violent winds."

Why Newfoundland was known as "Bacalaos"?

Newfoundland became known as "Bacalaos" or "Codfish-land" because of the rich fishing grounds off the Canadian coast.

What the name "Mississippi" means?

The Mississippi River flowed through the lands of many tribes—Fox, Kickapoo, Iowa, Winnebago, Miami, Oto, Chickasaw, and many more. Their names have been borrowed to name the states, cities, towns, and rivers of what would become the United States. Each tribe had a different name for the great waterway that runs like a backbone through the middle of the continent, but it was the Algonquin name "Mississippi" that stuck. It means "Big Water" or "Father of Waters."

Where the names Virginia and Louisiana came from?

Virginia and Louisiana were named after royal patrons. It became the custom for explorers to name newly claimed lands in the new continent after their royal patrons in the hope of continued favor. The earliest English colonies were established in Virginia, flatteringly named for Queen Elizabeth I, the Virgin Queen. De la Salle claimed the whole of the vast Mississippi valley in the name of Louis XIV of France.

Where the name El Dorado came from?

El Dorado or "The Golden One" was a legendary chieftain covered with gold dust, who washed in a sacred lake every evening. This legend lured the Spanish Conquistadores on an endless quest for gold in the New World. In time, El Dorado came to mean both a city of gold, and, as now, simply a dream of riches forever out of reach.

Who named the Grand Canyon?

Before the Europeans traveled across North America, this area was inhabited by Native Americans who had settlements in the canyon and its caves. The Grand Canyon was named in 1869 by a one-armed geologist, John Wesley Powell. He made the first journey by boat down the Colorado River that has carved out the canyon. His expedition consisted of nine men and four boats. Traveling 994 mi. (1,600km) and surviving turbulent rapids, deadly whirlpools, capsizing, and near starvation, most of his party fought its way through the huge canyons ". . . which unite to form one grand canyon, the most sublime spectacle on Earth." Their journey took 98 days.

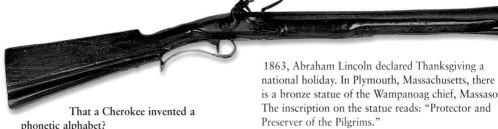

That a Cherokee invented a phonetic alphabet?

In 1821, Sequoyah invented a phonetic alphabet that had 86 characters. This allowed him to write down the Cherokee language. By 1825, most Cherokees were literate and, in 1828, the Cherokees started publishing the *Cherokee Phoenix*, the first Native American newspaper.

Which white man was made a Native American chief?

In the 1830s, a remarkable English missionary named William Duncan settle among the Tsimshian tribe of the Northwest. He started a Christian co-operative community, and eventually became the chief.

That some Native Americans were forbidden to speak in court?

The state of Georgia passed a law in 1828 that forbade Native Americans to speak in court, even in their own defense.

Where Colombus is buried?

Columbus died on May 20, 1506, at his home in Valladolid in Spain. In 1513, his body was moved to a monastery in Seville. It is said that in 1542, Colombus' remains crossed the Atlantic Ocean to Hispaniola and he was buried at the cathedral of Santa Maria in Santo Domingo. However, it is also claimed that his body lies in Havana or the cathedral of Seville.

Where the tradition of Thanksgiving Dinner comes from?

In 1622, the Mayflower Pilgrims, helped by the Wampanoag tribe who lived nearby, managed to bring in a good harvest. Half the Pilgrims had died in the winter of 1621, so in 1622, they joined in the Native American annual "Thanksgiving" ceremony. The custom continued and, in

1863, Abraham Lincoln declared Thanksgiving a national holiday. In Plymouth, Massachusetts, there is a bronze statue of the Wampanoag chief, Massasoit. The inscription on the statue reads: "Protector and Preserver of the Pilgrims."

Why Sioux warriors danced the ghost dance?

As the white man took over, the Native American population was gradually forced to live as farmers on special areas of land named reservations. Life on the reservations was hard. Many Sioux warriors began a "ghost dance" to persuade the Great Spirit to restore the old way of things. The dancers wore ghost shirts, that they believed would protect them from the white man's bullets. Just after Christmas 1890, the army arrested a group of about 350 ghost dancers and took them to a place named Wounded Knee. There they shot 180 men, women, and children. This was the last attempt at Native American resistance.

How Navajo women were able to spin a story?

Navajo women believed that they had been taught to weave by a spirit called Spider Woman, and they handed down both the skills and tools from mother to daughter. During the 19th century, white traders forced the weavers to use chemical dyes and imported fibers, but after 1920, the Navajo weavers returned to using vegetable dyes. They use symbols of lightning and sunbeams in their design today as they did in the past.

GLOSSARY

alliance A group of people, countries, or groups that share certain goals and agree to work together.

ambush A surprise attack by people lying in wait in a concealed position.

ancestor A person from whom one is descended and who lived several generations ago.

astrolabe An astrolabe is an instrument that was used to determine the altitude of objects (like the sun) in the sky. It was first used around 200 B.C. by astronomers in Greece. The astrolabe was replaced by the sextant.

backer A person, institution, or country that supports something, especially financially.

bearings Position in relation to other things; sense of direction.

besiege To surround with soldiers in order to attack or capture.

brave A warrior among the Native American tribes.

buckskin The skin of a deer.

cairn A mound of rough rocks built as a memorial or landmark, typically on a hilltop or skyline.

cape A piece of land that sticks out into a large body of water.

carpenter A person who builds or repairs houses and other things made of wood.

caravel A type of two- or three-masted sailing ship developed in the 1400s by the Portuguese.

cartographer A map maker.

cartography The science of drawing maps.

census A usually complete count of a population that normally includes social and economic information.

colonization The act of establishing a colony.

colony A place where a group of people come to settle which is under the control of their home country.

commerce The buying and selling of goods or services.

commodity Something that can be bought and sold.

compass A compass is a device that always points north. It is used for navigation.

compendium A collection of things.

contemporary Existing or living at the same time; belonging to the same era.

continent Earth's land masses are divided into seven large landmasses called continents. Earth's current continents are: Africa, Antarctica, Asia, Australia, Europe, North America, and South America.

descendant One who comes from a given ancestor or ancestors.

draftsman A person who makes detailed technical plans or drawings.

empire A group of nations or peoples ruled over by a powerful sovereign or government.

epitaph An inscription on a tomb or monument about a person buried at that site; a poem or tribute in praise of a deceased person.

fertile Producing or able to produce farm crops, or other plant life.

fjord A long, narrow ocean inlet that passes between high and rock banks or steep cliffs.

fleet A group of navy ships under one command.

geography Geography is the study of Earth's surface.

glacier A glacier is a slowly-moving river of snow and ice.

hide The skin of one of the larger animals such as a buffalo or cow.

homestead Land and buildings where a family makes its home.

hydrographic The science of the measurement, description, and mapping of the surface waters of Earth, with special reference to their use for navigation.

immigrant A person who moves to another country from his or her native land.

land rush This usually refers to an event in 1889 when the previously restricted land of the United States was opened for homesteading.

landfall Landfall means to approach, sight, or reach land.

legacy Anything that is passed down from ancestors, or someone who came before.

legend A story that has been handed down from an earlier time. Many people know these stories, but they cannot be proven.

longitude Distance on Earth's surface east or west of an imaginary line on the globe that goes from the North Pole to the South Pole and passes through Greenwich, England. Longitude is usually measured in degrees.

luxuriant Thick and healthy.

macramé The art of knotting cord or string in patterns to make decorative articles.

map A map is a representation of a place. There are many different types of maps that have different uses.

maraud Roam in search of things to steal or people to attack.

mariner A seafarer or navigator on a ship.

merchant One who buys goods and sells them for a profit.

migration Movement from one region into another.

moccasin A soft leather shoe or slipper without a heel.

mustang A small, hardy horse of the American plains, descended from Spanish stock.

myth A story or group of stories that form part of the traditional knowledge of a society.

mythology A collection of myths.

naturalist A person who studies the natural world, especially plants and animals.

naturalistic Derived from real life or nature, or imitating it very closely.

navigation The act of setting a course for, or controlling a ship.

New World The New World is another name for the Americas (or the Western Hemisphere).

Northwest Passage A water route connecting the Atlantic Ocean and the Pacific Ocean across northern North America.

ore A naturally occurring solid material from which a metal or other useful substance can be removed.

outpost An outlying settlement.

pack ice Large pieces of ice that have been driven together to form an almost continuous mass.

patron A person who supports someone, a cause, or special event; explorers were often supported by the money and goodwill of the king or queen of their country, and acted as the representatives of their patron on their voyages to other lands.

peninsula An area of land almost completely surrounded by water except for an isthmus connecting it to the mainland.

pioneer Someone who is one of the first in a culture to explore or live in a place.

plains Level areas of land.

plunder To steal from by force.

pueblo A house built of adobe or stone, usually many-storied and terraced; often built against cliff walls, with entry through the roof by ladder.

rapids Rapids are parts of a river that are shallow, rocky, and have strong currents.

republic A nation in which those who make the laws and run the government are elected by the people.

settler A person who moves to and settles in a new country or area.

sponsor To finance or support a project or event.

stark Severe or bare in appearance or outline.

strait A strait is a narrow channel of water that connects two larger bodies of water.

temperate Of a moderate temperature, not subject to prolonged extremes of hot or cold weather.

territory An area of land that belongs to and is governed by a country.

tithe A tenth of annual produce or earnings, formerly taken as a tax for the support of the church and clergy.

trade The buying and selling of goods and services.

trading post A station or store established by traders in a sparsely settled area to barter supplies for local products.

tropical Very hot and humid.

uncharted Not mapped or surveyed.

FURTHER READING
& WEBSITES

BOOKS

America's Horrible Histories #03
Elizabeth Levy (Scholastic, 2002)

Atlas of Exploration
Andrew Kerr and Francois Naude
(Dorling Kindersley Publications, 2008)

Early Explorations: The 1500s (Hispanic America)
Roger E. Hernandez
(Marshall Cavendish Children's Books, 2008)

Explorer (DK Eyewitness Books)
Rupert Matthews (DK Children, 2005)

Explorers and Exploration
Steadwell Books and Lara Rice Bergen
(Heinemann Library, 2001)

Exploring North America
Jacqueline Morley (Peter Bedrick, 2002)

European Settlement Of North America: 1492–1763
(A Primary Source History of the United States)
Guy Francis (World Almanac Library, 2005)

History Pockets: Explorers of North America
Mike Graf (Evan-Moor Educational Publishers, 2003)

New York Public Library Amazing Explorers:
A Book of Answers for Kids
Brendan January (Wiley, 2001)

Pathfinders of the American Frontier: The Men Who
Opened the Frontier of North America, from Daniel
Boone and Alexander Mackenzie to Lewis and Clark
and Zebulon Pike (Exploration and Discovery)
Diane Cook (Mason Crest Publishers, 2002)

Tools of Navigation: A Kid's Guide to the History and
Science of Finding Your Way (Tools of Discovery)
Rachel Dickinson (Nomad Press, 2005)

WEBSITES

http://academickids.com/encyclopedia/index.php/
Daniel_Boone
An encyclopedic biography of Daniel Boone.

http://academickids.com/encyclopedia/index.php/
Henry_Hudson
An encyclopedic biography of Henry Hudson.

http://academickids.com/encyclopedia/index.php/
Lewis_and_clark
An encyclopedic entry on the Lewis and Clark
expedition.

www.civilization.ca/cmc/explore/virtual-museum-of-
new-france/the-explorers
The Canadian Museum of Civilization website which
contains information on the French explorers who
came to America.

www.eduplace.com/kids/socsci/books/applications/
imaps/maps/g5s_u2/index.html
An interactive map showing the exploration of North
America (1492–1700).

www.elizabethan-era.org.uk/christopher-columbus.htm
Timeline, facts, and a history of Christopher Columbus
and his voyages.

www.ibiblio.org/expo/1492.exhibit/Intro.html
An Exhibit of the Library of Congress, Washington,
D.C. The exhibition examines the first sustained
contacts between American people and European
explorers, conquerors, and settlers from 1492 to 1600.

www.kidport.com/REFLIB/UsaHistory/Explorers/
Explorers.htm
Information on early explorers including Columbus.

www.kidskonnect.com/subject-index/16-history/
265-explorers.html
A gateway to sites about the different explorers.

ww2.mariner.org/exploration/index.php
A useful website from the Mariners' Museum which
looks at exploration through the ages. Includes
information on the explorers, ships, tools of
navigation, and voyages.

http://pbskids.org/bigapplehistory/early/topic1.html
Click on the timeline to explore early New York
history from before 1600 to 1857.

www.floridahistory.com/
Spanish explorations and conquests in North America.

INDEX

A

Aiontwatha (Hiawatha) 9
Algonquin 21, 42
Amundsen, Roald 4, 33
Anasazi 8, 12
animals 21, 29, 30, 34
Appalachian Mountains
   30, 31

B

Baffin Island 18, 23
Bierstadt, Albert 7
Bjarni Herjolfsson 4, 12, 13
Boone, Daniel and
   Nathan 4, 30–31

C

Cabeza de Vaca,
   Álvar Núñez 4, 22
Cabot, John 4, 19, 22
California 19, 22, 28
Canada 29, 32, 40, 41
Cape Cod 12, 13, 27, 42
Carson, Kit 37
Cartier, Jacques 4, 23, 24,
   42
Champlain, Samuel de
   25, 31
Charbonneau, Toussaint
   35
Cherokee 43
Chesapeake Bay 21, 26
   27, 31
Choctaw 11
Clark, William 4, 34–35
Cole, Humphrey 19
Colorado River 23, 34
Columbia River 23
Columbus, Christopher 4,
   6, 8, 14–15, 16–17, 19,
   20, 43
Comberford, Nicholas 27
Conestoga Wagons 37, 39
Coronado, Francisco
   Vásquez de 4, 22, 23
Corps of Discovery 34, 35
Cree 41
Croatoan 26
Cumberland Gap 31

D

Dare, Virginia 23, 26
Davalos, Felipe 9
Declaration of
   Independence 31

Drake, Sir Francis
   18–19, 23
Drouillard, George 35
Dutch East India
   Company 29

E

England 18, 19, 25,
   26–27
El Dorado 42
Erebus (ship) 33
Erik the Red 12, 13

F

Florida 19, 20, 21, 31
Fox (ship) 33
France 24
Franklin, Sir John 4, 32,
   33, 34
Frémont, John Charles
   4, 34, 36, 37
Frobisher, Martin 4, 18,
   23

G

Georgia 30
Gjoa (ship) 33
gold 6, 18
Grand Canyon 23, 42
Great Lakes 25, 31, 37
Great Plains 22, 38
Great Slave Lake 29
Greenland 12, 13, 18, 40,
   41

H

Harding, Chester 31
Hiawatha 9
Hicks, Edward 26
Hispaniola (La Isabela)
   16
Homestead Act (1862) 39
Hudson Bay, River, Strait
   28, 31, 32
Hudson, Henry 4, 28–29,
   31
Hudson's Bay Company
   28, 31
hunting 10–11

I

Independence, Missouri
   39
Inuit 8, 13, 40
Iroquois 9

J

Jamestown 26, 27, 31
Jefferson, Thomas 34
John Barrow, HMS 33

K

Kentucky 30, 31

L

La Salle, René-Robert
   Cavelier de 4, 25, 31, 43
Labrador 13, 42
Lake Champlain 25, 31
Leif Eriksson 12, 13, 26
Léon, Juan Ponce de 4,
   19, 20, 21
Lewis, Meriwether 4,
   34–35, 37
Little Wolf, Chief 39
Louisiana 25, 31, 34, 42

M

Mackenzie, Alexander,
   and River 4, 29, 31
Matthew (ship) 19
Mayflower (ship) 27, 31, 43
Mesa Verde 8, 13
Mexico 20, 22, 23, 38
Mississippi River 23, 25,
   34, 42
Missouri River 31, 34, 35,
   37, 39

N

Narragansett Bay 19, 24
Native Americans 8–9,
   10–11, 16, 24, 27, 30,
   35, 36, 37, 38, 39
Navajo 43
Nevada 36
New Albion 19, 23
New Amsterdam 29
New England 12, 30
New France 25
New Mexico 23
New World 6, 14, 15, 16,
   17, 21, 27
New York, and Bay 19,
   24, 29, 41
Newfoundland 18, 42
Niña (*Santa Clara*)
   (ship) 17
Norsemen 12–13, 20
Northwest Passage 23,
   32–33
Nova Scotia 18

O

Oklahoma 22
Oregon and trail west 34,
   36–37, 38–39

P

Panama Canal 33
Parry, Edward 33, 34
Peru 20, 22
Pike, Zebulon 34, 38
Pinta (ship) 17
Plimoth Plantation 26, 31
Ponce de Léon, Juan 4,
   19, 20, 21
Powell, John Wesley 42
Provincetown 27, 31

R

Raleigh, Sir Walter 26
Roanoke Island 23, 26, 27
Rocky Mountains 7, 34,
   35, 36
Ross, John 32
Russell, Charles Marion 36

S

Saint Lawrence River 23,
   25
Saint Louis 35, 37
San Francisco 23
Santa Maria (ship) 17
Sioux 9, 43
Smith, John 26, 31
Smith, W Thomas 33
Soto, Hernando de 4, 20,
   21
Spain 14, 16, 20, 22
Speedwell (ship) 27
Straits of Belle Isle 13
Straits of Magellan 19

T

Terror (ship) 33
Thanksgiving 43
trade 18, 24, 25, 28, 29

V

Verrazano, Giovanni da
   4, 21, 26
Vespucci, Amerigo 4, 6, 21
Vikings 8, 12, 13, 19
Virginia 23, 26, 27, 30, 42

W

White, John 21, 26, 27
Wilderness Road 30, 31

ACKNOWLEDGMENTS

The publishers would like to thank: Graham Rich, Jan Alvey, and Elizabeth Wiggans for their assistance and David Hobbs for his map of the world. Picture research by Image Select.

Picture Credits: t=top, b=bottom, c=center, l=left, r=right, OFC=outside front cover
AISA: 6bl, 34c, 24/25c. AKG (London): 6tl, 10/11c, 17tr, 18bl, 21b, 32/33c, 36/37 (main pic), 38bl, 38/39c, 39br, 42bl, 43br. Architect of the Capitol: 20/21c. Art Resource: 10tl. Bridgeman Art Library: 7t, 16/17c, 18tl, 28tl, 35tl, 35tr. Charles Walker images: 12bl. Corbis Images: 21c, 24tl, 35br. Fotomas Index (U.K.): 7br, 18/19b, 21tr, 27cl, 33tr, 35/35c, 39cr. FPG International: 17cr, 22/23b, 38tl. Giraudon: 17bl, 14tl, 14/15, 15ct, 18/19c, 20bl, 26tl, 26/27b, 32bl. Giraudon/Art Resource NY: 24/25(main pic), 26/27t. Haschehoug & Co.: 33br. Hulton Getty: 10/11t. Image Select: 2, 8tl, 12/13t, 16b. iStock: 41br. Mary Evans Picture Library: 8/9t, 12/13c, 16cl, 26bl, 27bl, 28bl, 29c, 30/31c, 36tl, 37tr. Missouri Historical Society: 34/35b. National Gallery of Art: 24t. National Geographic Image Collection: (Felipe Davalos) 9cr, (Sisse Brimberg) 13br, (Bill Strode) 31c, (Randy Olson) 30cl, (James Sugar) 16tl. National Museum of American Art, Washington DC/Art Resource NY: 39tr. National Maritime Museum: 19br, 33bl. NHPA: 19ct. Photri: 11cr. Pix: 1, 28/29c. Planet Earth Pictures: 23c. Rijksmuseum-Stichting Amsterdam: 6/7c. Shutterstock: OFC. Telegraph Colour Library, U.K.: 12cb.The Granger Collection: 22bl, 23t, 29br, 29tr. The Hispanic Society of America: 21t. Werner Forman Archive; 3, 8/9b, 8bl, 9br, 9tr, 42t.

NOTE TO READERS
The website addresses are correct at the time of publishing. However, due to
the ever-changing nature of the Internet, websites and content may change.
Some websites can contain links that are unsuitable for children. The publisher
is not responsible for changes in content or website addresses. We advise
that Internet searches should be supervised by an adult.